# Grief

## RESOURCES FOR BIBLICAL LIVING

Lou Priolo, series editor

# Grief

*Learning to Live with Loss*

## HOWARD EYRICH

**P&R** PUBLISHING
P.O. BOX 817 • PHILLIPSBURG • NEW JERSEY 08865-0817

Printed in the United States of America

ISBN: 978-1-59638-203-9

# What Is Your Grief Story?

John found the love of his life when he found Mary. Almost from the first date, there was no doubt in their minds that God meant them for each other. A year later they were married. If you listened, you soon discovered that for them life began when they met and married. Three children and ten years later, Mary was given the diagnosis of pancreatic cancer. Within four months, John buried her.

Julie and Perry were married almost ten years when they finally adopted Jacob. All efforts to become pregnant had proven futile. Jacob was born to a fourteen-year-old girl who agreed to give him up, so that he could have a normal family. Julie and Perry were elated! Nine months later Julie found Jacob dead in his crib.

Sally was the life of the school. She was a cheerleader. She was president of the girl's drama club. A well-known Christian university awarded her a full academic scholarship for her 4.0 GPA accentuated by AP courses. As she was returning home from a basketball game, a drunk driver swerved into her lane and hit her head-on. Sally was DOA at the hospital. She was the only daughter of a highly decorated Marine who had been killed in Afghanistan in the mid-1990s. Her widowed mother had now been stripped of her entire family.

A veterinarian friend called Howard and said, "I have a great dog for you at my hospital. I think she is just what you want. Bring your family over for a cookout tonight, and you can take her home." When they left that evening to return home, Howard put Penny, a copper-colored mixed shepherd, in the back seat of the pickup truck with the children. She immediately rested her feet on the back of his seat and extended her face beside his. It was obvious that there was an immediate bonding between them. They lived on a busy country road, so Howard instructed the family not to allow Penny to run free until she could be trained to avoid the road. One summer day as he returned from work and pulled in the driveway behind the pickup truck, Howard noticed Penny's collar on the tailgate and some dark stains on the bed of the truck. He called out, "Hey, where is Penny?" His son called back from his upstairs bedroom, "Penny is dead, Dad!" Howard picked up Penny's collar and threw it as far as he could, and then made his way to David's room. There he asked David, age seven, what happened. David told him how Penny had been hit and that Mom had buried her. Howard knelt by David's bed, laid his face on David's chest, and wept.[1]

Jethro and Marybeth had a wonderful family of four daughters and one son. The four daughters were born early in their marriage, while Nehemiah Jethro was born the year Marybeth turned forty. NJ (for "new joy"), as his sisters dubbed him, was an all-American kid. He lettered in four sports in high school while maintaining a 3.5 GPA. He was awarded a Congressional appointment to West Point, where he graduated with honors. Jethro and Marybeth could not have been prouder of their boy. After graduation from West Point, he served in Special Forces, where he again quickly became a leader. He was sent to Iraq, and on his first mission he sacrificed his own life to save his men and was awarded the Congressional Medal of Honor.

1. This is my personal experience. Penny was the third dog I lost in my lifetime. The first was when I was six. Shep had been my playmate as long as I can remember. Since there were no children in the neighborhood, Shep was very special to me. The day I learned he died, I wept for twenty-four hours. When I was fifteen or sixteen, Trooper went berserk and snapped at me in the kitchen. I coaxed him outside, whereupon he ran away and never returned. All three losses were significant, and each was accompanied by grief. In each case, I lost a very dear "friend."

Tim and Joan were blessed with two girls and two boys. Their two girls flourished, but their two boys tarnished the family name. Neither boy took an interest in spiritual matters. Tim, Jr., was killed in a gun fight with the police at a failed bank robbery. Six months later, Joseph died of a drug overdose.[2]

I don't know the source of your grief. You may have lost a loved one, or you may be attempting to minister to someone who has. Perhaps the grief you are experiencing is not over the loss of a loved one. Rachel grieved over her closed womb (Gen. 30:1–6). David grieved over the isolation of Absalom (2 Sam. 13:37). Both of them failed to process their grief in a manner that resolved it while maintaining their integrity. Rachel gained a child by her handmaiden Bilhah, but found no resolution. David allowed Absalom to return from exile, but found no resolution (2 Sam. 14:24). As I was working on this booklet, a friend wrote to me the following personal experience:

> Last week, when we had to put our fourteen-year-old Ger-
> man shorthair, Charlie, to sleep, I was truly grieving. He
> and I were "joined at the hip," as they say, and I cried all
> weekend. . . . I'm sure there are people who would think it
> foolish of me to compare my sadness with the grief they feel
> at the loss of a loved one. I would differ, just for the sake
> of argument. It occurred to me that I was grieving more for
> Charlie than I had for my Mom, who died fifteen months
> ago. (Maybe I'm in denial?) And we were very close. I would
> be ashamed to admit this, except that I know where she is,
> and God has given me, quite literally, that "peace that pas-
> seth understanding" over Mom's death.

In the space allotted, I will not attempt to satisfy all your longings. I will, however, lay out for you an approach for dealing with grief that is biblical and different from other approaches to which you may have been exposed.

2. These are fictitious stories representing a variety of realities with which most readers will be able to identify to some extent.

It has been my experience over the years, when talking to those who have lost a loved one, that most of the guidance they received to process their grief mimics that of the world. Far too often Christians are confused and do not handle grief well. Our thoughts about grief have been greatly impacted by the world.[3] As a general rule, the local church has not sufficiently prepared believers for grieving. Christians are attached to life in the body. Our focus is too often not on things above. Too often our eyes are not fixed on Jesus (Heb. 12:2). We may sing "This world is not my home, I'm just passing through," but the reality is that we want to experience life in the body as much as possible, as long as possible, and as deeply as possible.

In the original languages, the Bible uses several different words that we translate as "grief" or "grieving." When I studied these different words, it quickly became apparent to me that the key to understanding the biblical role of grief is not going to be discovered merely by an examination of word usage.

But God has not left us without instruction on this important dimension of life that sooner or later becomes the experience of every one of us. Until I was fifty-two years old, I did not lose anyone close to me who was not at the end of a good life and had not reached the biblically allotted threescore and ten. Then my best friend died of cancer at forty-eight. It was a traumatic experience. He spent most of his adult life overseas flying for Wycliffe Bible Translators. He was called back to the U.S. to take up an administrative post. We were both excited at the prospect of getting to see each other frequently and going on hunting expeditions together, as we did when we were teenagers. However, before our plans could be realized,

3. A small group leader in our church called me for guidance in dealing with a member of the group. It seems that during a Bible study this member blurted out her anger at God over the fact that she had recently been diagnosed with MS. "I don't understand why God is doing this to me!" she exclaimed. She was grieving the loss of her health. Rather than processing this tragic reality through the biblical perspective of the love of a sovereign God who had given her the promise to "work all things together for good," she was following the pattern of the world by slipping into anger.

he was taken from me, and I knew for the first time what it felt like to lose a loved one prematurely. My mother, on the other hand, lost seven children. Four of them were late-term pregnancies before she turned twenty-one. Your loss is your reality, just as my loss was my reality. Most of us would think of my mother's losses as almost intolerable. But they were her losses—and they were tolerable.

So, what is grief to us as believers? How do we define it? How do we describe it? As I did the word study mentioned earlier, I found a common element in the references I consulted. It is this: pain! It is felt physically. It is felt emotionally. It is felt spiritually. Sometimes our bodies hurt as our souls agonize. Sometimes we feel like we will burst from the pressure of our emotional turmoil. Sometimes we feel spiritually numb—as though God were not there. Grief is a complex of experiences. It cannot simply be characterized as a series of predictable stages. It is impossible to order the dimensions of the experience in a linear fashion. For example, a person may not experience anger at the loss of a mate immediately following the funeral. However, nine months later, when certain tax irregularities cause serious complications with settling the estate, anger may become a real issue. We cannot simply move from one stage (denial) to another (anger), proceeding through the sequence. Grief is an individual experience, not a predetermined psychological maze through which everyone necessarily passes. It is not a social phenomenon. It is a uniquely complex experience, not a routine series of simple steps.

Well, then, how is the Christian to experience grief? I would like to walk you through the Scriptures and sketch for you the elements of Christian grieving.

To do this, we begin with the church at Thessalonica. This is a church that Paul planted. Paul writes to them—commending them, encouraging them, and answering questions that they have raised about the Christian life. One of those questions has to do with those who have fallen asleep—that is, died (1 Thess. 4:13). Paul begins with the reality: the Thessalonians will no longer have them in their lives. He affirms their grief, but he limits it, "so that you will not grieve as do the rest who have no hope" (4:13). Next he outlines the reason for not grieving as the rest grieve. Paul writes: "For if we believe that Jesus died and rose again, even so God will bring with Him those who have fallen asleep [died] in Jesus" (4:14). He ties the limits of our grief to our own personal faith. In other words, if we are believers, then our grief is limited by our faith. Since I believe that I and all other believers will be raised from the dead, then I cannot allow my loss to encumber my life with crippling pain and sadness. In other words, through the indwelling power of the Holy Spirit, I must choose to limit the effects of my grief. As in all other aspects of life, in dealing with grief Christians do not appropriate the power of their faith with the same spiritual dexterity. However, the message of the apostle Paul is that we do not have to experience grief in the same way as those who have no hope. We know that Jesus has removed "the sting of death" and replaced it with eternal life (1 Cor. 15:54–57). We also know that he has given to us the Comforter. Hence, we have confidence regarding our loved one, and we have solace for our souls as we adjust to our loss. It is now a matter of appropriating these spiritual verities in our lives.

If our loved one was not a believer, what then? How do we process the grief? I believe that we rest in the sovereignty of God (see Ps. 139:14; Rom. 9:1–6, 18–21). Ultimately each individual is responsible to believe the Gospel message. In John 1:12, Jesus said, "But as many as received him, to them gave he power to become the sons of God, even to them that believe on his name." In John 6:44, this same Jesus said, "No man can come to me except the Father which sent me draw him" (KJV). So when we lose a loved one whose relationship with God is questionable, we must accept the reality that his or her eternal destiny is dependent on one side upon the reception or rejection of Jesus, and on the other side upon God's initiative to draw him or her to himself.[4]

4. Two days before my father died, I stood at the foot of his bed while he rested in a semi-comatose state. I prayed, "Father, I am hopeful that in his closing hours of

"Okay," you say, "then I am to be a zombie and have no feelings!" No, such is not the case. I want to lead you through an exercise and then examine biblical models of grief and look at how believers can process it effectively. As we do, we will see that we are to face reality, to express our emotions, to honor those who have died, to talk about them, and then to move forward with our lives!

## Facing Reality

We face reality by asking the simple question, "Why do we grieve?" Let me suggest six reasons why we grieve. (There are probably other reasons as well.)

*1. We grieve because we are separated from what we have lost.* When my son was six, we moved from Pennsylvania to Georgia. We moved away from the only house, home, community, and friends he had ever known. He left his best friend, David. It took my son the better part of a year to adjust to the reality of this separation. The separation from his woods, his creek, his house, his church, and especially his friend, was a deep experience of loss. For my six-year-old son, his friend David, for all practical purposes, had died.

*2. We grieve because of the fear of the unknown.* One of the questions that is often heard in the confusion of a new loss is, "What will I do?" It may be a mother who just lost the father of her three young children. It may be the employees who just learned that the owner of their company was killed in a plane crash. It may be the church whose pastor was just killed in a mountain climbing accident. It may be the father who just lost

_____

consciousness, Dad repented and turned to you as did his sister on her death bed. I take comfort knowing that he heard the gospel on many occasions. Amen." I then rested his eternal destiny in the sovereignty of God.

his leg in a traffic accident. Unfortunately, we too often do not identify the root of the question, which is fear.

*3. We grieve because of our anxiety.* I know a family in which the husband and father was killed in a freak accident. This man had not planned well. He had no life insurance and no investments. His wife left college as a freshman to get married, and was left with practically no marketable skills. She asked again and again, "How will I take care of myself and the children?"

*4. We grieve because of guilt.* We have all heard a tragic story in which a husband and wife or a father and son have a terrible argument and say things to each other that are hurtful and destructive, and afterward one of them learns that the other was killed shortly after the argument. The one left behind often lives with agonizing guilt over the words said and the missed opportunity to mend their relationship.

*5. We grieve because we think we have to grieve.* One of my personal practices, when a friend sustains a significant loss, is to visit him or her two or three months after the loss. I have two reasons for doing so. The first reason is that after the first six weeks or so, many other people have forgotten about the loss. I want the friend to know that someone is still thinking about him. The second reason is that by that time, often the friend in this situation has actually made a reasonable adjustment to his new reality, but is concerned that others will think poorly of him if he appears not to be grieving. If I hear this somewhere in our conversation, I affirm him in his adjustment and encourage him to continue embracing his reality. If a spouse or child has died, I generally encourage the friend to postpone any major decisions for another eight to ten months, so that he can have a year-long perspective on his new situation.

*6. We grieve because of the loss of the loved one.* We grieve what he or she could have been. We grieve the incompleteness of a life project. We grieve the trip we did not get to take together. We grieve the loss of companionship—the laughs, the frustrations, the habits. If my wife were to precede me in death, I would definitely miss her smile, her face reaching over to kiss me good night, her empathy with my work, her nurturing of our adult children, and her grandmothering skills. I would miss the wonder of our connectedness in the various dimensions of life. Actually, there are a thousand other bits and pieces of warmth that I would miss. Those experiences of her would be sweet memories and the source of tears periodically shed during the rest of my life.

Have you noticed something as we have tiptoed through these emotions? Have you noticed that they are about us, not about the person or the place or the pet that was lost? I don't grieve for the person who is lost, but for my own resultant loss. In grief, God gives us temporary permission to focus on ourselves. As we shall see, he gives us permission to ask the questions and work out the answers. In our Christian-influenced society, and even in most pagan societies, people give each other space and time to grieve. And that is as it should be.

## Learning from Biblical Models

We will now look at four different types of grief modeled by figures in the Bible. We will consider their reactions to their loss, and see what we can learn from their example.

### 1. Abraham—Loss of a Spouse

Genesis 23 records the death of Sarah at 127 years of age. Abraham was approximately 137 at that point in time. Here is what we learn. In verse 1 it is recorded that Abraham mourned for Sarah and wept over her. He freely expressed his emotions at her loss. Sometimes the expression of our emotions can be very strong and even frightening to those around us. My first funeral after moving to a new pastorate instructed me in this regard. I was asked to travel with the father of a young woman who had died. On the trip to the grave site, the father wailed in a manner outside of my personal experience. His wife, who was considerably younger than he, was embarrassed. The Lord gave me the insight to comfort her by explaining that her husband was expressing the depth of his emotional pain and that this was perfectly acceptable. Interestingly, that trip to the grave site was the first step in a relationship with this man that eventually led to his salvation.

After Abraham expressed his emotional response to Sarah's death, he proceeded to arrange for her proper interment. Reading the rest of the story in chapter 23 gives us some interesting instruction. Abraham was concerned for the security of Sarah's resting place. This no doubt was the outgrowth of his conviction of the coming resurrection (Heb. 11:10). It was also an expression of his honor of Sarah. Following her burial, Abraham engaged his servant by an oath to secure a wife for his son Isaac in their home country. While the text does not say so, there is reason to see this as honoring Sarah (cf. 24:67). Yet Abraham was unwilling to compromise his call from God to leave his father's land and go to the place that would become the Promised Land (24:8) in order to obtain a wife for Isaac. He kept his perspective of keeping God first. Rebecca did indeed return with Abraham's servant and marry Isaac. Abraham himself appeared to have worked through his grief by this time, and he married Keturah and began to raise another family.

So what do we learn about grieving from Abraham? (1) Mourn, that is, weep—express your grief. (2) Honor the lost loved one. In this case, he gave her a proper burial. (3) Honor reasonable commitments. I recently counseled a woman whose mother made her promise not to let her father remarry for at least one year. That was an unreasonable demand, because this woman did not have the authority (she did not have control of her father's choices) to exercise this responsibility. Abraham recognized that his servant could not force a young woman to return with him and marry Isaac, so he told his servant that he would be released from his commitment to bring her back if she was unwilling to come with him. (4) Proceeding with one's life does not dishonor the loss—in this case, the deceased wife. For example, when my son got over the loss of his friend when we moved to Georgia, he did not thereby dishonor his friend.

### 2. Joseph—Loss of a Father

When Jacob was near death, he gathered his sons around him and pronounced his blessing upon each one of them (Gen. 49:28). After that, "he drew his feet into the bed and breathed his last" (49:33). Then Joseph, like Abraham, wept over his loss. Like Abraham, he arranged for a proper burial to honor his father. In this case, he adopted the manner of preparation utilized in Egypt. Jacob had asked for a reasonable promise (50:5), which Joseph arranged to fulfill. However, in this story we have an added element. Both his family and the Egyptian community supported him by entering into the process with him. Following the burial, Joseph moved forward with his life and honored his father by forgiving his brothers for their evil deeds toward him.

One of the most exciting truths of Scripture is that of forgiveness. This story describes what our present culture would refer to as a very dysfunctional family. Biblically, we see that it was filled with sins—lying, manipulation, desire to murder, pride, and favoritism, to mention a few. But Joseph, after his father's death, found the freedom of forgiveness. His brothers could now live without the fear of retribution. Joseph was free from resentment and hatred. Joseph could have jailed or executed his brothers. But he had already decided to forgive them, so that when they approached him, he could affirm their forgiveness (Gen. 50:15–21). Forgiveness is a truth that many grieving people need to embrace. It brings freedom (see Rom. 12:16–21)!

### 3. David—Loss of a Child

Our third model is drawn from one of the saddest stories in the Bible. King David failed to be occupied with God's business.[5] As a result of his idleness, he gazed upon a married woman and lusted after her. Being the king, he commanded that she be brought to him. Remember, kings were absolute. A king's word could mean life or death. Bathsheba complied and became pregnant (2 Sam. 11). David attempted to cover his sin by enticing Uriah, her husband, to sleep with her. Being a man of integrity, Uriah refused to do so while the military unit he commanded was on the battlefield. David, who under other circumstances would have given Uriah a commendation for his sense of duty, was incensed that his sin might be discovered. He sent Uriah back to the battle and instructed the field commander to place Uriah in the heat of the battle and then withdraw, leaving him to be killed. The dastardly deed was accomplished (11:23–24). But David did not succeed in covering his sin (Pss. 32, 38, and 51). God sent Nathan the prophet to unmask him (2 Sam. 12:1–15). Months later Bathsheba delivered and subsequently the child became ill at the hand of the Lord (12:15).

David entered a time of prayer and fasting (12:16). But the child died (12:18). Upon hearing that the child was dead, David arose, bathed, and ate—to the amazement of his comforters. When questioned about this strange behavior, David responded, "While the child was still alive, I fasted and wept; for I said, 'Who knows, the LORD may be gracious to me, that the child may live.' But now he has died" (12:22–23). Then David asked two very instructive questions: (1) Why should I fast, now that he is dead? (2) Can I bring him back—will my fasting and praying change

---

5. The complete account may be found in 2 Samuel 11–12.

anything, now that God has revealed his will? David answered his two questions with two very instructive facts: (1) I shall go to him. (2) He will not return to me (12:23).

Following this interchange, David returned to daily life. At the appropriate time, he slept with Bathsheba and she bore another child, Solomon (12:24). David returned to his duties as the leader of his army (12:28–29).

So what do we learn about grief from David in this situation? First, we pray fervently for the healing of our loved one, but we submit to God's will. Second, we recognize that many losses (like death) are permanent. We cannot change the situation. Third, we reengage with our loved ones who have been impacted by the loss. Fourth, we need to engage in the responsibilities that God has given us and not let the grief protract our distraction from his service.

The loss of a child can be a terrible blow. It is a blow from which people frequently do not recover. My cousin Bobby was four years older than I was. He married young, so that by the time I was in my third year of college he already had a five-year-old daughter. But his daughter died from a medical error. I tried on several occasions to comfort Bobby and share the gospel with him. From a grief-stricken heart filled with anger, he turned on me and said something like this: "You shut up about God or don't bother coming around!"

This grief burrowed deep into his soul, resulting in ever increasing self-indulgence that led eventually to divorce and the abandoning of his other children.

David's loss was the result of his terrible sin. Bobby's loss was the result of someone else's error made in good faith. David was confronted and confessed his sin. He petitioned God to spare the child, but accepted the reality of the loss. He did not become paralyzed by guilt and returned to his God-given responsibilities. Bobby refused to forgive. He refused to accept his reality and adjust. In the process, he poisoned the lives of all who loved him and who were part of his life.

## 4. Mary and Martha—Loss of a Sibling

The fourth model is not just about siblings dealing with the ultimate loss and the accompanying grief. As we will observe, this incident offers us some strong spiritual medicine. Perhaps the most important lesson to learn from this story is the fact that our grief, our personal pain, is about much more than our agony, our process, or our recovery. It is about learning truth—truth that can transform our lives, truth that enables us to embrace a reality that is beyond space and time, beyond loss.

In John 11, we have the story of two sisters and a brother who are close friends of Jesus. Lazarus was seriously ill. The best doctors available told the sisters that he was not going to make it. They had seen Jesus heal many people, so the answer was simple: send for Jesus! But when they sent for Jesus, he purposely delayed his arrival (11:6). He informed his disciples that this illness was about "the glory of God" (11:4). When they finally departed, Jesus informed them, "Lazarus is dead, and I am glad for your sakes" (11:14–15). When they arrived, Martha was very upset. She exclaimed to Jesus, "If you had been here, my brother would not have died" (11:16). Does that not sound like what one of us might say if we could not reach our doctor in time to save our loved one? Jesus then proceeded to instruct them regarding the resurrection and the fact that he himself is the resurrection and the life. You remember the rest of the story. He raised Lazarus.

God has strong spiritual lessons for us in this incident. First, his glory takes precedence over our emotional pain and loss. It might be better said that God intends to transform our emotional pain and loss into his glory. Second, truth is more important than life. Jesus was willing to let Lazarus die in order to communicate truth. He was not lacking in compassion, however, for the Scriptures tell us, "Jesus wept" (11:35)! Here we see the heart of Jesus for each of us who experiences the ravages of sin in the death of a loved one. In this case, Jesus raised Lazarus from the dead, but it would only be a matter of time until he died again. The raising of Lazarus (11:43–44) was not the resurrection of which Jesus had spoken (11:23–26). It was only a temporary resurrection. While this temporary resurrection was of great concern to Martha (11:22), Jesus was focused on illustrating the eternal resurrection in this situation.

## A Biblical Way of Processing Grief

When I was in high school, Nate Saint and his fellow missionaries were killed by the Auca Indians. The wives and families of these men suffered deep emotional pain and real loss. The Christian world was upset. In 1955, even the secular world was upset at this news. Could Jesus have sent angels to prevent this massacre? Absolutely! Their lives could have been spared. When the news arrived back at the mission base camp, did the widows and children think, "If the Lord had been there, my husband and Daddy would not have died?" I suspect that some similar thoughts occurred. I also suspect that some well-meaning fellow believers said something like, "I am so sorry, but you know that God is in control." Right doctrine, but wrong timing! In retrospect, would any Christian today (and likely most of those family members) doubt that the massacre was within God's plan for his own glory? I think not, because God has allowed us to see how his plan played out. The gospel has spread among these Indians as a result, and there has been a salutary impact upon the families.

I once observed a family in which an ideal young man, fourteen or fifteen years old, accidentally killed himself. When I went to the viewing, there were hundreds of high school students waiting in line. It took a couple of hours for me to get to his parents by the casket. While waiting, I watched them minister to many of the youth. When I left, the line was as long as it was when I first stepped into it. This young man was obviously highly regarded by his peers. While I am sure that tears still come to his mother's eyes from time to time as she remembers her son, I am also sure that if you asked her about it, she would affirm that this was within God's plan and that he received glory through this painful situation, while many others benefited through coming to an understanding of the gospel message.

How long should the period of mourning and grief be? Again, there is no place in Scripture that prescribes a particular period. However, returning to Paul's first letter to the Thessalonians, it would seem that the key to narrowing our grief to the point of resolution is how we rest in Jesus. There are three practical steps that will assist us in this process.

*First, we must practice processing grief.* Everyone has frequent opportunities to face and process grief. Sometimes it is as simple as updating our computer. While there is always an anticipation that accompanies my triennial computer update, there is also the sadness of giving up something with which I've become very familiar. It is almost like giving up an old friend. Men reading this will identify with the idea when it comes to a car. Perhaps for women it will be parting with an outfit that has been a favorite. When we bought our current house, the woman who had lived there before us experienced grief. She had personally decorated it, room by room. Learning to deal with these small grief experiences appropriately trains us to deal with the more difficult challenges.

The loss of a pet through death, or just having to give it up, is an opportunity to practice processing grief.[6] Several years ago I had a nostalgic hankering for a dog. My wife listened carefully,

6. This is one of many reasons for children to have animals. The loss of a pet gives them an opportunity to learn the meaning of death and separation. They learn that death is not something we control, either in terms of time or manner. They learn about loss, pain, disappointment, an empty feeling, unanswered questions, and the value of others standing with them, encouraging them, listening to them, and talking them past the hurt. They can learn to pray about their hurt and to trust God to enable them to adjust.

researched a particular breed, and gave me a Border collie for Christmas. I quickly fell in love with Shea. After six or seven months, my vet informed me that Shea, being a work-dog, needed a job to do and that this explained her incessant barking. I would not have wanted my neighbors to do to me what I was doing to them—having a dog in my yard that spent many hours a day barking at everything she could find to chase and who seemed to make up things to chase when she could not find something. I determined that Shea needed to move to a farm. This was not an easy decision, however. She had become my furry friend who came to meet me when I came home, no matter what time it was. She would sit beside me while I stroked her and watched TV. I grieved the separation!

These small but real losses in life provide the opportunity for us to learn to deal with grief in a biblical way. For example, we can learn to adjust to the loss, rather dwelling on it and falling into a pattern of self-pity.

*Second, we must practice theology proper.* Theology proper is the study of the nature or character of God. Understanding that God is sovereign (in control of everything), omniscient (all-knowing), loving (that he sought us out even when we were his enemies), and omnipotent (all-powerful) enables us to see God as greater than our grief experiences of life. I am a minister, an educator, and a counselor. When my son washed out of college his first semester, I was deeply grieved. My solace was found in practicing my theology proper. I knew that God loved me and my son. I knew that God was powerful enough to work in my son's life to bring about the changes necessary for him to succeed in life. I knew that God knew what was going on in my son's head and heart. And I knew that God was sovereign, so my son's wash out was not outside of his plan. It took four years to see God's hand played out in his life. Today he is a graduate of the University of Georgia and is a landscape architect who, with his partner, owns his own company.

*Third, we must practice practical adjustment to the realities of life.* There are at least six components to this process.[7]

1. In the midst of grief, we must be patient and make important decisions carefully. We have all heard a horror story like the one in which a widow sold her home and moved to Florida three months after her husband died, only to sell the Florida home and move back eighteen months later, $30,000 poorer.

2. Be committed to growing. There is an old adage that says we are either growing or dying. The injunction of the apostle Paul is that we are to grow in Christ. Situations of grief can be opportunities for expansive growth if we have an attitude adjustment.

3. Extinguish bitterness and the desire for revenge quickly through forgiveness. Only we can determine not to allow the one who caused us hurt to continue to control us through that hurt. A man I once saw in counseling was angry with his father years after his father had died. His anger was associated with his grief. His father had died before he graduated from college and left him without the means to pay for his education. As a result, he did not graduate, and felt he was always underemployed as a result.

4. Establish realistic goals. Don't determine that you are no longer going to cry when you think of your pet, your house, your father, your spouse. My mother has been dead since 1976, but I sometimes find tears filling my eyes when my grandchildren are around and I think about how much she would have enjoyed them.

5. If necessary, for a time, consider a principle that Jesus articulated in Matthew 5, the principle of radical ampu-

7. I say *at least* six because there may be a number of others, depending upon the source of grief, one's knowledge of Scripture, the depth of one's personal walk with the Lord, and the demands of life (such as a woman having to return to work while still having children to raise).

tation. Perhaps it may be necessary for you to put away pictures or other constant reminders for a period of time. I would advise putting them all away, except for one by your bed. If you put them all away, you may find that you induce a struggle with guilt for doing so. Remember, I said that this section is about being practical.

6. Write out a prayer in somewhat formal language, which you can use to pray about your struggle with your grieving. Then, when you come to your personal time with the Lord each day, read this prayer before the Lord and thereby limit the time and energy you invest in the struggle. It is very easy to develop a pity party or simply to indulge in an emotional release that leaves one exhausted and excuse it as prayer.

We experience other kinds of grief besides the death of a loved one. We have focused on such grief here, since it is the most obvious form of grief. However, as I have mentioned, there is grief associated with losing a job, a broken marriage,[8] or the loss of a home in a fire, hurricane, flood, or tornado.[9] There is also grief associated with a doctor's diagnosis of an incurable or irreparable condition. Grief is a companion in this fallen world. Even as I write this booklet, I have a friend who suffered a serious bout with cancer, which the Lord miraculously healed.

8. Here are the words of a friend who went through a divorce: "I know how I suffered for several years during and after the divorce process and how helpless I felt. Suddenly and unexpectedly, I had lost my closest human friend. She wasn't dead, but she was out of my life, even though I saw her frequently with her new love and, eventually, husband, because we had joint custody of my daughter. Also, suddenly my home and financial security were threatened and it took several years to recover financially." Sometimes this grief is worse than the grief of losing a spouse to death. It is compounded by betrayal and rejection, which must be faced regularly as one proceeds with one's life.

9. I watched my mother grieve at the loss of our farmhouse to fire. Her loss was compounded by the fact that her treasure trove of my dead sister's dancing gear burned in that fire. She grieved the loss of my sister again after nearly forty years. I also watched my father, who lived with us, succumb slowly to Alzheimer's. I grieved little by little. The day he died I felt relief—and then guilt for feeling that way.

Yet she grieves for her companion in treatment, who recently was told that her cancer had returned and spread to her lungs. Another friend lies in a hospital bed with his life hanging in the balance. I grieve over his situation, knowing that I may not see him again in this life.

So, as you read this booklet, I trust that the message is clear. Whatever the source of your grief and the accompanying struggles may be, it is in the biblical approach to that grief that you will find hope and help. One model is provided by the apostle Paul, whom God left to live with a thorn in the flesh (2 Cor. 12:7–10). It is a biblical model that can be applied to many of our situations of grief:

1. He asked the Lord to remove it three times, and the answer was no.
2. He had the Lord's promise, "My grace is sufficient for you."
3. He found a new attitude in acceptance and could say, "I am well content with . . ."

Finally, if you are struggling with grief over the loss of a loved one, let me suggest returning to 1 Thessalonians. As you do, remember the model given by Paul to the Thessalonians:

- We know where the loved one has gone.
- We know we cannot change the destiny of those who have died.
- We know that there are answers to our questions because we have confidence in God (though sometimes the answer will have to wait until eternity).
- We know the promises of God.

With these thoughts in mind, focus on Jesus and develop your trust in him, with regard to both the departed loved one (and all other lesser grief experiences) and your own functioning. Here are some parting thoughts to keep in mind:

- Put off:
  1. Fretting, that is, anxiety about yesterday (Ps. 37:1).
  2. Anxiety about tomorrow (Matt. 6:32–34; Phil. 4:4–9).
  3. Anger at God, the other person, or yourself (which may come in the form of guilt or blame, resulting in depression) (Eph. 4:26, 31).
- Put on trust in the living God, who is the God of the good news (John 3:16), who is in control and who desires to *lead you through* this loss with his knowledge and power (Ps. 23). Psalm 23 is the love note of your Savior. His love is expressed in the wonderful promises of this psalm. These promises are based upon who he is! He is the Good Shepherd, who protects, feeds, and cares for his sheep.
- Renew your mind (thinking) regarding God, and see your loss through the eyes of the God of comfort. The Hebrew word *nacham* is translated some sixty-five times as "to comfort" or "to be comforted." It is the word used in Scripture for being consoled over death. In 2 Samuel 12:24, it is the death of an infant. In Genesis 37:35, it is the death of a teenage son. In Genesis 24:67 and 38:12, it is the death of a mother. In Isaiah 66:13, a mother comforts her child, and in Psalms 71:21; 86:17; 119:82; Isaiah 12:1; 49:13; 52:9, God comforts his people. Remember the declaration of the apostle Paul that God is "the Father of mercies and God of all comfort" (2 Cor. 1:3).
- Remember that the Holy Spirit is the Comforter (John 14:16) and makes intercession for us with groanings that cannot be uttered (Rom. 8:26). It is said of Jesus on various occasions that he saw people's suffering; he had compassion on them and healed them. The Greek

word *splanchnizomai*, "to be moved with compassion," is related to the word for bowels in Greek. It speaks of a very bodily experience, that is, of one's physical and emotional engagement. Hebrews tells us that Jesus was tempted in all points as we are (Heb. 4:15). Remember, Jesus felt his grief, so he can understand how we feel our grief.[10]

May the Lord bless you and keep you. May the Lord make his face to shine upon you and give you peace. This is God's good word, his benediction!

10. Note that all three members of the Trinity are involved in our comfort: God the Father is the "God of all comfort" (2 Cor. 1:3). God the Son, Jesus Christ, experienced our temptations as he passed through intense grief, and therefore can comfort us (Heb. 4:15–16). God the Holy Spirit is called by Jesus "another Comforter," who comes in his place (John 14:16 KJV).

# Appendix A: Don't Feel Like You Are Stuck If You Don't Go through "Stages of Grief"

JUST WHAT IS a stage of grief? It has been my experience over the years, when talking to those who have lost a loved one, that most of the guidance they received to process their grief mimics the world's wisdom. Too often Christian writers have either turned directly to secular writers or turned to Christian writers who have resourced secular writers. When I was in graduate school, Elisabeth Kübler-Ross was in her heyday. She was a medical doctor who took a great interest in death and dying. She updated and elaborated the work of Erich Lindemann.[1] Her five stages of grief can be summarized in the following manner.

- *Denial*: "This can't be happening to me." "I refuse to believe this!" This is a normal, initial response to crisis.
- *Anger*: The individual is no longer denying the incident, but rather is expressing anger about it. Why? Why? Why?
- *Bargaining*: "God, if you will do this, I will do that."
- *Depression*: The unhappy realization sets in that nothing can be done about what has already happened.
- *Acceptance*: The person realizes that what is truly important is his or her response to the incident.[2]

1. Erich Lindemann did an extensive study of families of the victims of the Cocoanut Grove nightclub fire in Boston in 1942.

2. These stages are repeated today in most books discussing grief.

An astute contributor to Wikipedia made the following observation:

> It is essential to set the record straight, once and for all, about the *constant misuse of the stages* that Elisabeth Kübler-Ross defined in her book "On Death and Dying." The stages she created [actually, they are behavioral phenomena she observed] *are the possible stages* that a dying person "might" go through, upon being told they have a terminal illness. *They are not the "stages of grief"* as would be felt or perceived by a grieving person who is reacting to the death of someone important to them. *In fact, there are no such stages.* Individual responses to the impact of the death of a loved one—or less than loved one—are as unique and varied as humanly possible. *Any attempt to codify those reactions into a simplistic set of emotions is dangerous and limiting to the griever.* At The Grief Recovery Institute [www.grief.net] we have been working with grieving people for 27 years. We have yet to meet someone in "denial" that a loss has occurred. Almost always, their opening comment to us is to tell us exactly what the loss has been: "My mother died," or "My husband left me," or "My son was killed." There is not an ounce of denial in any of those comments. We can equally dismiss the other "stages" as not applicable to grieving people.[3]

We would do well to heed the warning that it is "time to stop promulgating false ideas and using incorrect language."[4] The popular media and other sources speak of the Kübler-Ross stages of grief as scientific fact. However, her conclusions were based upon observations of people who were informed that they were terminally ill. At best, her stages could be descriptive of what a dying person *might* go through upon being informed of his or her terminal condition.[5] Furthermore, a right rela-

---

3. www.Wikipedia.com, cited 12/23/06 (emphasis added).
4. www.Wikipedia.com, cited 12/25/06.
5. Kübler-Ross did not say that a person *must* go through all these stages, nor did she indicate that there must be a specific *order* of stages. She concluded that a person must go through at least *two* of the stages.

tionship with Jesus Christ was not, to the best of my knowledge, taken into consideration. This factor is too significant to ignore.

What has been disturbing to me over the years is how often this secular philosophy has been uncritically absorbed by Christian writers and made the standard for Christian "grief work," as it is often called. The sequence and pattern must be worked through. If it is not, then the griever will supposedly "get stuck" in the grief process. This process, we are told, is "normal"—meaning that everyone must go through it in some degree. For the non-Christian, such a patterned process *may* be the pathway to acceptance of, or adjustment to, reality.[6] However, the believer, with the hope of resurrection and eternal life, need "not grieve as do the rest who have no hope" (I Thess. 4:13).

Recently I was mentoring a doctoral student through a practicum. He sent me a worksheet that he had given to a woman who was going through grief. It listed the five stages cited above and asked the woman to identify where she was in this normal process. I wrote the following to him:

Let me suggest some things for your consideration.

1. Can we really say these are "normal"? Normal suggests "right" or "should." I find it difficult to embrace the idea that bargaining with God is a "should."
2. While denial may be the first response, I think a better term is "confusion" or even "disbelief." It is not so much "I refuse to believe this" as it is "How do I process this?" or "What does this mean for me?" or "How could this possibly happen to . . . ?"
3. Is anger a "should" for the believer? Is anger always a necessary step?

6. In recent years, there has been some corrective brought to this issue in the professional realm. However, at the popular level (where most grieving people turn for help) the idea persists that these *are* the stages and they *must* be worked through.

4. Depression signifies a tendency toward some form of "dysfunction." Is this a "should" for believers? Would it not be better to speak of confusion and disorientation or disorganization? These conditions certainly mimic the face of depression.

The bottom line is that Christians, on the whole, do not handle grief well. We have been greatly impacted by the world, as seen in the discussion above. As a general rule, the local church, through its regular preaching and teaching, has not prepared believers for grieving. Christians are too attached to life in the body. Our focus is too often not on "things above." Too often our eyes are not fixed on Jesus (Heb. 12:2). We may sing "This world is not my home, I'm just passing through," but our reality is that we want to experience life in the body as much as possible, as long as possible, and as deeply as possible. We all need a good dose of Paul's thinking that "while we are at home in the body we are absent from the Lord" (2 Cor. 5:6).

As a result, we Christians are all too often not satisfied with the solace and comfort offered in the Word of God. We turn to the world to seek a practical understanding of our grief and the grief of others. Thus, we focus on working through our anger at God or the lost loved one, rather than confronting our anger and realizing that it is the result of our judging of God (for being unfair in taking our loved one) or the departed one (for "leaving us in this mess"). We should seek wisdom from God to sort out the mess and utilize our energy in cleaning it up.

Bargaining with God is not a defensible tactic. Presumably the followers of Kübler-Ross place the depression stage after bargaining because the bargaining is unsuccessful and therefore the individual spirals downward into depression. We see a few times in Scripture where God reversed a death, but in none was it the result of negotiation (1 Kings 17:17–24; Matt. 8:5–10).

It is neither deserving nor natural to spiral down into depression because we are grieving. As one walks through the Scriptures, especially the Psalms, it becomes clear that depression is the consequence of sin (unless biological in origin), not grief.[7]

Kübler-Ross's final stage, acceptance, is certainly a realistic goal. In a general sense, the Christian would agree that this is a significant aspect of grief.

For a Christian, there are three broad dimensions to grief. These could be called *stages*, but I prefer *dimensions*. The word *stages* suggests an orderly progression. However, these three dimensions do not necessarily follow in order. They usually look more like the following diagram.

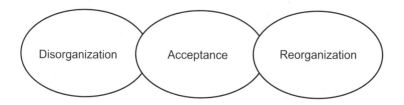

These three dimensions are:

> *Disorganization*—A relationship is deconstructed. The orderliness of life is distorted. There is often an infusion of entangled responsibilities. (See John 11:21–46.)
> *Acceptance*—There is the realization that life will never be the same again, coupled with a willingness to engage the new frontiers of life. (See Luke 24:13–35.)
> *Reorganization*—The individual will make the choice to honor God, others, and self by the reconstruction of relationships, life structures, and responsibilities.[8] (See Acts 1:12–26.)

7. See Wayne Mack, *Out of the Blues* (Bemidji, MN: Focus Publishing, 2006).
8. I do not claim originality for these terms. Jay Adams used two of them when writing about grief. However, I am not aware that anyone has used them in the

Where do you see evidences of these dimensions in your own life? Take some time to fill in the lines below.

Disorganization: _____

_____

_____

_____

Acceptance: _____

_____

_____

_____

Reorganization: _____

_____

_____

_____

As indicated in the diagram, one should not expect simply to pass from one dimension to another. However, one should expect to vacillate from one dimension to the other. Usually, in the case of a death, this process will last approximately one year. There are many dynamics that will impact the time factor. For example, the children of a sickly parent who has lived a long, productive, and enjoyable life can typically move through their grief more quickly and easily than the parent of a perfectly healthy child killed in an auto accident.

In cultures where there is an established process for marking the end of grief, people adjust and go forward. In our culture, where such an accepted process does not exist, scholars differ on how long the grieving period should last. Some people suggest three months to a year, while others argue for extended periods for some people. It has been my experience

---

manner that I have. See Jay Adams, *Shepherding God's Flock* (Grand Rapids: Zondervan, 1986), appendix A.

over forty years of ministry that three months to a year tends to be the norm.

As Christians, we see these three dimensions connected by God, as illustrated by the diagram below. We see him in control at all times. We see him as loving, protecting, caring, and consoling at all times. We are seeking wisdom, understanding, and enablement. We are trusting him—the omniscience, omnipotent, sovereign, and all-wise God who loves his people. We acknowledge that we do not know his plan, but we rely on his character and power for his plan to be worked out in our lives for his glory and our benefit.

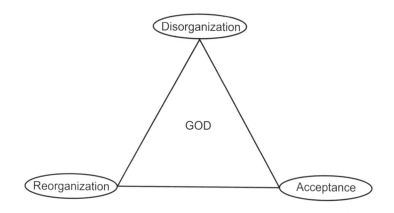

Our help and hope are not found in working through the secular stages of grief, but in allowing ourselves to experience our emotions while processing our loss in a biblical manner. This processing is accomplished by working through the disorganization of our lives toward acceptance and reorganization. It is imperative that we do this through a conscious relationship to our loving heavenly Father, who has promised us the ultimate hope of resurrection and life with him (1 John 3:2).

The disorganization phase includes a variety of possible emotional experiences, such as guilt, anger, and depression.

However, you should not anticipate any particular one of these emotional responses. Rather, you should seek to address *your experience* in accordance with God's Word. Here is where the assistance of a biblical counselor (pastor, Sunday school teacher, friend, or counselor) should be sought.

# Appendix B: Don't Let Sorrow Fill Your Heart[1]

BEFORE HIS DEATH, Jesus gave his disciples some disturbing information. He told them not only that the days ahead would involve considerable difficulty, but also that he would no longer be with them. For quite some time, these men had had a special relationship with the Lord and a very real hope that he would be establishing his kingdom on earth in the immediate future.

How did they respond when they realized their hopes were about to be dashed? Their hearts were filled with sorrow. "But because I have said these things to you, sorrow has filled your heart" (John 16:6). The word *filled* implies a kind of filling that is complete. It is to fill to a full measure—or, as we might say, to fill to the brim. When something is completely filled, there is room for nothing else. When a heart is filled with sorrow, that sorrow so completely occupies one's life that it displaces everything else.

Now there's nothing wrong with a little sorrow. In fact, Jesus was "a Man of sorrows and acquainted with grief" (Isa. 53:3). Yet he also had an abundance of peace, joy, and love. He was able to say such things as "My peace I give to you" (John 14:27), "These things I have spoken to you, that My joy may remain in you, and that your joy may be full" (John 15:11), and "As the Father loved Me, I also have loved you; abide in My love" (John 15:9). So a certain amount of sorrow may coexist with love, joy, and peace in one's heart.

1. The material in this appendix has been adapted from Lou Priolo's book *Losing That Lovin' Feeling* (Wetumpka, AL: Pastoral Publications, 2003), 81–86. Bible quotations in this appendix have been taken from the NKJV.

Jesus never let his sorrow prevent him from fulfilling any of his responsibilities. That is, he never allowed his sorrow to become so great that it totally shut him down. "Now My soul is troubled, and what shall I say? 'Father, save Me from this hour'? But for this purpose I came to this hour" (John 12:27).

In the garden of Gethsemane, Jesus told his disciples, "My soul is exceedingly sorrowful, even to death. Stay here and watch with Me" (Matt. 26:38). He then proceeded to pray so agonizingly that "His sweat became like great drops of blood" (Luke 22:44). His disciples, on the other hand, allowed their sorrow to keep them from fully discharging the responsibilities he had just given them:

Coming out, He went to the Mount of Olives, as He was accustomed, and His disciples also followed Him. When He came to the place, He said to them, "*Pray that you may not enter into temptation.*" And He was withdrawn from them about a stone's throw, and He knelt down and prayed, saying, "Father, if it is Your will, take this cup away from Me; nevertheless not My will, but Yours, be done." Then an angel appeared to Him from heaven, strengthening Him. And being in agony, He prayed more earnestly. Then His sweat became like great drops of blood falling down to the ground. When He rose up from prayer, and had come to His disciples, He found them *sleeping from sorrow*. Then He said to them, "Why do you sleep? Rise and pray, lest you enter into temptation." (Luke 22:39–46)

The disciples were exhausted as a result of their sorrow. Yet Jesus admonished them for sleeping and commanded them to get back to work. When we are faced with any loss, it is normal for us to grieve. As Solomon said, "Sorrow is better than laughter, for by a sad countenance the heart is made better" (Eccl. 7:3).

The danger comes when we allow our grief to become so great that it overpowers other things in our lives that God says we ought not to let slip. When experiencing heartaches, we can easily allow sorrow to fill our lives to such an extent that we stop thinking about those things that generate love, joy, peace, and the other fruit of the Spirit. Our sorrow must not quench the Spirit's work in our lives. We ought not to grieve so much that we stop fulfilling our biblical responsibilities or avoid our opportunities for ministry. Rather than allow our sorrow to control us, we should continue to be controlled by the Spirit. To be "filled with the Spirit" (Eph. 5:18) is to be controlled by the Spirit. To be filled with sorrow is to be controlled by sorrow.

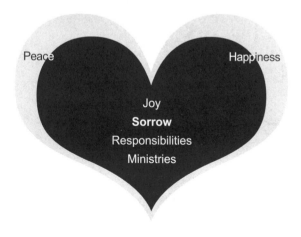

"But what if I'm already there? What if I've allowed my heart to be filled, or almost filled, with sorrow to the point that I'm shutting down mentally and emotionally?"

Then, by the Spirit's enabling power, you will have to work hard at getting your sorrow back down to a manageable level. First, think the kind of thoughts that will generate the right kinds of feelings. "Whatever things are true, whatever things are noble, whatever things are just, whatever things are pure, whatever things are lovely, whatever things are of good report, if there is any virtue and if there is anything praiseworthy—meditate on these things" (Phil. 4:8). Rather than thinking only of what you've lost, think about how God may be using your loss to benefit you. Rather than thinking about how miserable you are, ponder how you can make someone else happy. Rather than worrying about what will happen to you tomorrow, figure out how you can be a blessing to someone today. Instead of grumbling and complaining, praise God for all of the things he has done for you.

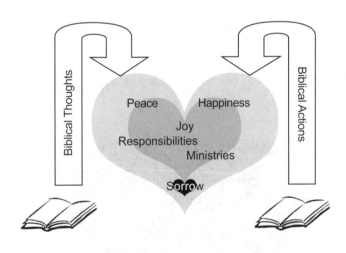

The second thing you can do to help get your sorrow under control is to fulfill your biblical responsibilities. If you are not already doing so, get involved in ministering to others. Yes, you can do these things even when your heart is sorrowful. It may not be easy, and it won't be fun at first. But in time your mind will be occupied with more noble thoughts than your own grief. The satisfaction that comes from being responsible, and the joy that comes from serving others, will begin to refill your heart, displacing your grief.

Take a few minutes right now to make a list of any respon-sibilities you've been neglecting as a result of being consumed with your loss. Then write out Philippians 4:8. List those things you can meditate on when you are tempted to think about all you've lost. Put this list in your wallet or purse and carry it with you wherever you go.